Tropical Depressions

Winner of the Iowa Poetry Prize

Tropical Depressions

POEMS BY ELTON GLASER

University of Iowa Press Iowa City

University of Iowa Press, Iowa City 52242
Printed in the United States of America
First edition, 1988

Book and jacket design by Richard Hendel
Typesetting by G & S Typesetters, Austin, Texas
Printing and binding by Braun-Brumfield, Ann Arbor, Michigan

Library of Congress Cataloging-in-Publication Data

Glaser, Elton.
   Tropical depressions.

   (The Iowa poetry prize)
   I. Title.   II. Series.
PS3557.L314T7   1988   811'.54   87-30205
ISBN 0-87745-200-8
ISBN 0-87745-201-6 (pbk.)

The author would like to thank the University of Akron and the Ohio Arts Council for granting fellowships that made the completion of this book possible. Grateful acknowledgment is also made to the following publications in which many of these poems first appeared: *Akros Review; Cape Rock; Chicago Review; Cincinnati Poetry Review; CutBank; Field; A Fine Madness; Garland Edition; Georgia Review,* "Fantasia on Tchoupitoulas Wharf"; *Hilltop; Icon; Iowa Review; Lips; The Little Magazine; Louisiana Literature; Mid-American Review; Ploughshares,* "Mosquito Hawks"; *Poetry Northwest; Poetry Now; Poets Ohio: The Art of the State; The Reaper.*

For my mother and father

Publication of this book

was made possible

by a generous grant

from the University of

Iowa Foundation

Contents

THREE

ONE

To have been born into a world of beauty,
to die amid ugliness, is the common fate of
all us exiles.

—Evelyn Waugh

Complaint against Crows

In the August cornfields, the crows
thin in winter, tumescent by May
lurch black and sleek as politicians.

I hate their icy hearts,
their dry, scrabbling feet.

They bore me
like the letters I sent long ago
complaining to you of love.

What do I complain of now?

These words
and the small defections of the mind.

The way the breasts
of women at sixteen
sweep back and forth in their gaudy halters
like radar.

Exile, a northern sun
scraping the windows, the palaver of leaves
from a strange tree, the wry
silence of snow.

The soft fall of money in another hand,
praise fitted and draped on another name,
peace expanding a worthier heart.

The inquisitions of the future,
the inquest of the past.

And these crows, these insolent crows
fat with satisfactions of the harvest,
beating their black wings against the grain.

Festive Songs on Lesser Occasions

You will die of the domestic.
—Jon Anderson

These beehive mornings, the hectic
Rising of the sun, butter and honey
Falling from distressed bread, and on the radio
Some over-the-counter-tenor or French horns
Blurry as trumpets with a three-day cold—

And soon the menopausal shower,
Hot flashes in the bathroom
As children work the basin faucets
Like spaceship controls, and I lift
Flaming towards that unfinished planet
Far above the hairy dregs of this day—

Until, out of the bourbon's backlash
And tobacco and last night's
Risorgimento in the sheets, I piece myself
Together and pull the necktie tight,
The knot so hard against my throat
I can feel the blood stop in its tracks
And turn back. And the world begins.

El Rancho Roacho

Dance this mess around.
—The B-52's

I know this place:
the bellhop with his heroin tattoos,
the keyclerk screaming the midnight
names of luck; the way they toss
each morning down the halls
a bucket of sawdust, soaking up
the poor man's gravy, enough
blood and mucus
to announce the birth
of some great beast that drools
at your doorsill, bringing
news of the new day.

It's always like this
at the taco motels,
the cantinas where skinny women
slide from their barstools
at the first rough touch
of their tits, where the mean boys
crouch in the alley, running
their blue blades over stone: all this
night labor longing for dawn.

I've given my fingerprints
to the city of lost angels, I sleep
with a ginshot hag that hates me,

I don't hang no picture frames.
Nine lifetimes past lunch, red-eyed,
one lung praying to cancer,
I pound my way back
through the alphabet, typing
with ten thumbs and a headbone
these pornographies for children,
the old sad pop-up books of love.
In this way, I pay for
the invention of the wheel
and every wreck that followed.

Bad afternoons, I race the dial
around the kilohertz, pulling
from the public air
a gangwar of drums and guitars,
anything to keep me
from thinking
of those sighs and grunts
in another room: is someone
coming or crapping
or easing the ache
that drives him through
the sliding noose of his dreams?

O I'm dancing the Apocalypso,
both feet on fire
and my eyes
sucking the light from the room.
I have seen God
with his pompadour and fruitboots,
his big rings banging
on the keyboard, and a voice
one decibel above brain damage
calling through the clouds:
Keep a-knockin'
but you can't come in.

My door is always
open to the hell of hard shoulders,
and I'll give you so much
grief and passion you can
start a new earth of your own,
all snarls and sweet whiskey
and something dripping you can't turn off.

Mal de Moi

When I see that summer moon
cranked up to heaven, and feel
a telltale rattle in the backbone,
corkscrew in the brain,
I go down these guilty streets
looking for someone low enough
to live up to—
        some sly eyeshadow,
a tongue that swings down
like a rat's tail between
two dislocated lips, whose business is giving
voodoo blowjobs for loot;
           or some citizen
improving his hours under the neon,
a face gone green and German,
saving the blade for me, a steel
keepsake in a slur of blood, working
from the hangnails in. Ah,
if this is life,
all jumpcut and slow dissolve,
I can leave it
but I can't
leave it alone, or stand here
in a suit broken on the rack, my head
bowed and bare to the passing weather.

One more time let me mole through
the alleys that mislead my feet
to Bonsoir the Hatter
who will, with his thimble
upright as a robot's condom, pull shut
the shades and fit me
in this small *chapeau,* a dream
with seven feathers roosting in the band
and a brim dipped continentally down,
until the mirrors all throw back
a face so farfetched and grand
it's like leaping on the queen's lap
at the opera, the royal box, overcome
by the flashpoint
of those high heroic arias
in a language I will never understand.

Ground Level

1

These plants can't live on love and dog piss.

Hibiscus, you know the moods of water,
How it broods and breaks and takes down
Each twist in the sun's conspiracies, too shifty
For the ferns and the weeping fig.

Mimosa, you've heard the alibis of light,
Sunbows over your African tassels, your leaves
Asleep in the half-truths of the moon
That only the backward rose believes in.

These plants can't live on wishes and the bad luck of birds.

2

It's that kind of weather, so weird
Even the newborn greens can't grow: the days droop
Like lizards on a warm stone
And the nights keep travelling, looking for
The lost motels on the star-map.

You see these bare shrubs mulling for a grubstake,
Bell peppers tolling in the wind,
And lilies polishing the pews on Sunday
When the sermons stick to the roof. . . .

3

And here comes that fool
With his sloppy boots and a chainsaw,
Wheezing and eager to bring the world back
To ground level, down to the brine and briars,
A human scale where the impatient teeth
Whittle even the air away, until the clouds
Hover over our heads like the blank balloons
Of a comic strip, panels in which
The people have nothing to say or think
And the joke is too painful to explain.

The Lesson

1

Students, in their sullen analysis,
pull the blood back
knob by knuckle and once more
drive their tired pens
through the heart of a poem.
Another inquisition of the trivial,
wrong answers
to the questions no one asked.
Another sick look
out the window, the panes
crusted with dust and the damp lines
from a thousand clouded brows.

2

I think Casanova once bent deep,
as they do, over
an unforgiving book, keeping
his neat accounts
after the spillage and farewells
silken with promises, pouring sand
on the lies, the brutal praise.
Perhaps, in his stone room, hiding
from the law or a lover's arms,

he felt a warm wind
tease the hair from his neck
like a woman's touch,
half-savage, half-civilized,
until he must turn
back to his stale page, longing
for someone else to betray.

3

Little shepherd of the book,
have all your sheep gone
over the stony end, putting down
a last backsliding adjective, or phrases
that look both ways
before crossing the mind?
Somewhere among them, I'm hunting
that blunt genius who
wasted on the walls of the men's room
I staggered through last night
his brave idiom, lifesize and naked:
My mother died in this bar.
He, too, shall pass.
Let the other bastards
repeat this lesson till they learn.

Corrosive Sublimate

With blindfolds and dope, with all the hairy pangs
Of honey eaten from a lion's head,

They woo the hazards, coax the foreskin back
In the brackets of a scratch-and-sniff hotel,

The Simian-Hilton, where the bellhop looks
Like an organgrinder's monkey in his pillbox cap,

And the torsos turn over when the clocks
Strike two, wrapping up

The half-hour honeymoon and the hot lunch.
I know how it is:

You want someone with the soul of Hogarth
And the hands of Norman Rockwell

To sanctify this scene,
An overlay of Boy Scouts on the debauchery,

And not simply to set down
The ache and pester of these days

That slide like butter in a scorched pan,
A hard white cream that clarifies

And then burns black.
Was there ever a green age

When the goatgod and his women
Tangled underneath the trees, wild flesh and horseflies,

The only music their split squeals
And someone's breath in a bonepipe,

Long before the Greeks began
To take themselves seriously,

All those noble speeches
Wiping up the backstage blood?

And now, for your sake, I'll take up
The slack, painting on a red smile

As if I were a whore who, after fucking,
Washes out her womb

With vinegar, rinsing in alum
Until the membranes pull tight

Around a snag of raw beef,
Lying like a virgin for your needs.

Hogtown Stomp

O you can sing the blues with the best of them, though you're not
blind or black and your kidneys still flush twice a day. When you
plug in your little amp and with a big thumb bend a scream and
stutter from the lowest string, all the bellies on the dancefloor
drop like erratic elevators. You hurt them till it helps.

One-man ghetto, blue eyes bleary from the smoke of burnt-out
lives, you buck and wing to your own rough tune as the platform
rattles and the sweat leaps off you like baptism in reverse. That
song about bad luck, that song about the amber mysteries of
whiskey, that one where the women pull back their long legs to
the vanishing point—every syllable cured in sour mash and
swept out by a slurred tongue! Mule of passion, you unload those
burdens until even the nights grow lighter and the days drive you
home at the end of the empty streets.

Elegant Solutions

I could never be confused with that man moved by his own music,
   that Adonis of the avenues, whose poems survive only in secret,
   in primitive abandon of the ballpoint on bodies that, for me,
   remain forever insurmountable—slant rhyme of the breasts,
   Lascaux of the labia. Nor do I in the least resemble that bard
   among cowboys, Slim Volume, who schooled his meters in the
   mesquite gaits of his nag, and nightly tested a leadpipe lullabye
   on the bulls, their big eyes blank as his verse.

Having thrown over all interest in cattle and pantoums and
   mysteries of the garter belt, I will consecrate myself entirely to
   the important questions of our time, such as: does Critical Mass
   define the number of murders one must commit before one can
   be properly acclaimed a mass murderer? Such as: does the
   nuclear-driven vibrator really constitute the first of the Six
   Warning Signs of God?

Pending the elegant solutions, I am going to visit all the forgotten
   places of this earth, including the gazebo and the mezzanine. I
   will be blessed among fishfries, consoled by parachutes, anointed
   with a local anaesthesia. In spite of the damage beige has done,
   in spite of the duckblind and the clipboard, I will continue my
   experiments with postminstrel depression, getting as much
   mileage as I can out of the wishbone, and conflating my
   headlong pleasures: to watch halftime ceremonies at the Enigma

Bowl, and to deconstruct nostalgias of the wet dream (always
alert to the afterglow of a peignoir, pajamas in a vapor lock).

And when I have made my peace with the lefthand hinges of this
allegory, and have arranged for the perpetual upkeep of the busy-
signal, I will purchase that small plot my years have hankered
for, and spend these last days humoring the dead, who have gone
the way of the inkwell and the napkin ring, and on whom I will
leave my mark in accents grave and acute.

Homage to Catatonia

I've lived so long on the business end of English, I can take
anything, even the woman I love, Hulga, who stands there in her
spandex pants, pointing a sharp finger at my heart, saying "I'll
freeze your assets, son. I'm gonna close *all* your accounts."

But tonight I'm feeling rangy as a leopard with his halfback hips,
I'm cranked up, I'm deep in the Gospel of Gratified Desire. All
over town, my syntax is raising the hair of strangers. And she
says, pulling off her blue inscrutable shirt, "You know, you have
the hands of a mutant."

Promiscuous syllables! Panoramas of the breath! I offer you this
deadpan stare, a brain nine years behind the news. Here in the
dry bowels of America, in a bedroom blocked by books and
tampons damp with her blood, I'm holed up like the last tourist
of the inward life, taking the woman I love, taking the lines of
least resistance.

Coming and Going

Whatever we get out of this,
It's not enough. Once,
I could rattle a flat highway
To somewhere else, on the front seat
A jug of monkey rum
And miles behind me a woman
With her heart blown out, soaking
The motel bed in moans,
As the moonlight fell
Face down in the parking lot.

After the wrong turns
That heaved us here, as far
From heaven as from hell,
We brood over the blame:
The unforgiving shifts of weather; a blur
Where the plot lines rise
Out of smalltalk into crisis;
Havoc in the maps. Looking for
The only road left open, the course
Of least grief, we try
To take it all back,
Like wheels sidewinding deep
In mire and loose gravel,
In the slack panic of regret.

But the way I feel tonight,
Neither misery nor mercy
Can steer me through the mudmaze
Or heal my needs. And already
It's too late for anger,
The kind that patches up
The wound it's opened, poultice
At the pressure point; too late
For apologies, the rearview retrieval
Of colliding lives. I want to
Put the pedal down again and leave
Blue smears and smoke
When I drive these shaken dreams away.

Wedlock

Jesus, help me
she cries, her knees bruised
on the bathroom tile, her curls
splashed over the porcelain
as sixteen years of agony
spill into the bowl, the first rule
of drinking lost hours before:
never mix bile with bourbon.

Some nights there's no telling
grace from disgrace.
And when Jesus can't come,
a spell of projectile vomiting
will soothe the soul.

Her needs are simple now—
a cool hand on the forehead;
words that will ease
the long way up, loosen
the locked jaw, and
fill her with herself.

But you're not the one
to save her; she's trembling
in your hands as if
you had found her once more
hiding from her crimes

and forced her, head bent,
to the block—cop and judge
and keeper of the breakneck blade.

And when you brush the sweat back
from the pale wreckage of her face,
you'll feel the same sick abyss
she drops through each morning
as you leave, taking
the whole day with you;
and you'll know, in the sour smell
of her kiss, how she recoiled
those angry midnights when you
offered on your lips
a backwash of tobacco and muscat women.

And now her eyes
slide back, empty
as the name you gave her,
as if she were looking through
the keyhole of hell, as if
face down in the toilet
she saw herself this time
inside the white fossil
of her bridal veil, draining
like an abscess, cleaning out
the small foul pool of her life.

[24]

New Year's Fear

A sudden wind between us shakes out
The match you lit the rockets with, the last one
Scorching through the sky, blue quench
And hoot, drizzle of small stars,
A new year's nova blown back to earth.

For blocks around us, the crackers spizz and boom
As if this were an Irish wake and time
Would rise out of its dead self to dance,
The good booze moving like the bowels of God.

But nothing changes in the end: it's still
All alibis and elegies.
               And yet
In this midnight blitz, I see
The fires praise your face, the brow burning,
Each cheekbone angled out in flame. You blaze
Crazy as a Chinese holiday,
A hundred torches dripping and licking
Over the dragons with human feet, those halfbreeds
That lash me back in line, unrolling the daredevil
Scare and lightning of their tongues.

I want to pull this night down over me,
Pillow my head on the useless moon,

Before the dawn storms through
The smoke and sex and chatter,
And every pledge we made starts breaking like the day.

Planting the Flag

This hand adventuring
between the sheets
may bring back
fresh encompassings,
silks and spices of the flesh.

But if there were sudden
errors in the wind,
or the stars' evasion, or a mind
snapping in the storm
like a white sail too tightly rigged—

would I still come
splashing to the shore,
this sinking sand and tangle
of dry vines from which
a wild red face
looks out
in awe and anger, and claim it,
planting the flag
in some higher name, as if
this were a new world mine to take
and not an island of its own,
already old and far from
the whispered riches of the East?

This hand will hold
what it can, because it can, making
the salt voyage home, keel high,
or full as the moon
that deepens and carries back
new latitudes of light, beyond
the birdcries and bellblare,
the green sleepwalking waves.

Primitives

No more than halfway out the cave
where the black wounds of bison
drip from the walls and the wheel
still rolls slowly towards us from the future,
I'm busy inventing the brake.
You can tell this
from the slump in my forehead, by the way
my hands tangle in their own loose hair.
But when my woman burns
her strange meat in the shadows—
something with feathers pulled down
on the hot savannah, or something with claws
plucked up from the sucking swamp—
I put by my tools and gaze, recalling
that scrink of flint, the sparks'
quick scatter in the dry wood.
And as the flames braid and waver,
I do the apeman dance, once more walking
on these ugly knuckles, hands clenched
against the earth, as if my infant senses
stumbled their first step in the new world.
O woman, when you fry
in that tatter of smoke, I know
there's no stopping, I can feel
my slow head bob and gnaw

like a blaze that feeds on what we breathe,
then licks itself clean, more mother to us
than those far waters aswarm with dirty life:
fire that is always faithful
to itself, always on the move,
bicker and sweet tongue
and the long backbends of love.

T W O

You've got to stop mocking—and start enduring—the
truth.

—Raeburn Miller

Storm Damage

Another bad night,
The rain speaking in tongues again
And the radio pulling through the purged air
Only some brimstone preacher
Hotwired from the wilds of Oklahoma,
That sooner-or-later state
Where all my sins will be healed
By five dollars and a baptism of dust,
As if Jesus had nothing better to do
Than ride shotgun all day in a pickup truck,
Blessing the oil rigs and the rodeos.

Oh it's a serious rain all right,
A nervous sobbing wreck, some sleazy angel
Drunk on his own grief and smearing
The windows with a wet face, while the wind
Does its falldown comedy, its vicious slapstick.
But I'm too tired to let these mysteries in,
Too washed out for any voice
That sweeps in sour against the freedoms
Of whiskey and money and painful women.
Let it all slobber down the drainpipes,
Slide out like grudges and black mud. I could

Drown in my own sleep, the big cold dreams
Closing over me, if not
For those long spikes of lightning driven in the sky
And those gusts that blow half the moon away
And that god-gossip wrangling through the trees.

Descripture

I've been reading the latest
cutrate testament, two books
trimmed back and patched into one,
the uplift updated
for the busy and the bored.

I kneel to that genius
who could divinely mix and match
until only the good parts remain,
spliced together beyond the logic
of theology or the scholar's art,
to keep the plot line moving
and hold no one back
by laws or lists or lamentations.

It's a hell of a story this way:
Noah loading up the ark
with a plague of frogs, of hail, of flies,
as the rising waters turn to blood;
Solomon, that wise miser,
splitting a baby in two, and those halves
hacked in half again and so on and so on,
until five thousand faithful were fed
on the infant's flesh, and only
the true mother threw up her meal;
and those four disciples

slapping their brows in astonishment
when, out of the great stinking fish
their nets had snagged and landed,
old Jonah stepped forth, still seasick,
still disgruntled, asking for
a shortcut back to Nineveh.

Each night, in the halo zone
of my lamp, I thumb through the passions
and obbligatos of belief, wrestling with
the messengers of God, reliving the miracles,
the foolproof promise of a second chance.
It's all here, set down
in the secret language anyone can learn,
decoding as quickly as Judas
who, according to this gospel,
was last seen lost
in the hanging bathrooms of Babylon
where, under those drawings
that massacre the innocents, he read
the handwriting on the wall:
For a good time, call Jesus Christ.

And thanks to this little black book,
I've got his number too.

Holograms of the Holy

When we build the new church,
we'll have this 3-D Christ
tacked up on the wall, the spikes
so close and clear we can almost
feel the sharp blood drip
on our special glasses,
the ones that make us look
like dictators from Bolivia or moviestars
at the bottom of a three-day drunk.
When we build the new church,
we'll pull out the pews and put in
some bucket seats with valves
and levers and swivel controls,
for those long novenas when we're all
kneebent and backbroke from toting up
the excremental repetitions of the litany.
When we build the new church,
our priest will come down in thunder
to the gospel bells, he'll ring out
his parables of power behind a pulpit
fashioned halfway between
the presidential podium and
the grillwork from a Coupe de Ville.
O there won't be nothing
good enough for us—
we'll wrap the altar rail

in aluminum siding and scrape
every stain out those stained glass windows.
And in the lobby, we'll build
a baptism basin big as a
Greek armpit-heater, so deep you could
drown a whole orphanage in it at one time!
But brothers and sisters,
we'll have no hand-holding hymns
when we build the new church,
no slim and sickly young men
swishing their catgut guitars to a holy yodel—
when we build the new church,
we'll wire in these new computer organs
that play nothing but the fugue states
of Bach, Bach as baroque
as a handshake in Harlem,
as fiery as brimstones sizzling
from the devil's piss, until
the whole nave is ablaze
with that good German knowhow,
beyond all miracles of the collection plate.

Syllabus of Errors

I

I still believe, the way an amputee still feels the leg he has watched
a surgeon toss in the bloody bucket. But will that pay my
admission to the other world, sweep me through the turnstiles of
purgatory, or out of hell, its only exit a revolving door? And from
which side will I watch the gates of heaven swing shut on a blind
hinge?

II

At the professor's funeral, we all stood sadly upwind while his body
cried out for the gift that was almost given. I would have brought
back his tongue, cured in lies and the droppings of minor poets,
but it was much too good for you.

III

Your sweet times have turned bitter in the brain, those nights of
arsenic for the lovers, those long afternoons dismembering the
saints. I will close them like books, asylums of memory where
summer is always slumming but the moon provokes no miracles
on the wrecked bed—nothing to disinherit, nothing to deny.

IV

I put out the lights of a waning year. Something slow moves
   through the city, some broken word that no one should hear, like
   old or *desire*. Through the dead streets, I carry a shovel with me
   to fill whatever has become empty in the night.

Dolls Divided

They were wood raised to the highest power, our features pressed against them like a fingerprint filled with blood from the victim's heart. But though we covered them in the morning with their dwarf clothes and undressed them each evening, we could never find in their smooth grain the hanging gardens of our father or what our mother hid between her legs, the only thing both sow's ear and silk purse.

And however often we laid them for the night between the pages of our books, marking the places we had abandoned for sleep, we would find them no wiser by morning. All those acres of oak brought down at the knees! Spines broken that the brain might live! We shook them and shook them—even God in his tantrums was not so angry!—until their heads came clear from their bodies, wreckage all around us, stupid and sexless and beyond repair.

Dolls Reading Descartes

They have the unencumbered look of cows that moment before the
sledgehead storms into the brain. Does nothing brew inside that
painted porcelain, no great thoughts steeping in their teapot
skulls? Good breeding will always tell, René. Old slugabed, in a
hot room you dreamed the world down to geometry and wound
up years later with a chill caught at dawn drilling metaphysics
into the Queen of Sweden, dead in that land of bears among the
rocks and ice—even you cannot disrupt these sailor suits and
pinafores, or make one glazed eye blink at your method and your
mathematics.

And yet, there is a crack starting in the cranium, just under the
horsehair toupees, and spreading like a new line drawn on the
maps when the treaties have all been sealed, another country cut
from a stubborn birth. Some deep pressure must be pushing
through the core, the dura mater laboring at last. They are trying
to think and it's killing them. O God, what horrors will back out
now—spiked wings whetted on the air, or white ooze circling a
sunset yolk like a bloodclot in heaven—when this eggshell
breaks?

Ragdoll Raga

Why should I complain of my birth? I was not built up from mud
or knocked into knobs and vents on a stolen rib. These stitches
were spliced in small and neat by a seamstress less frantic than
Herr Frankenstein, who laced up the square skull of his monster
like a cheap football. I was made new from castoff calico and
silk, diapers and denim, with a widewale spine of corduroy.
These are mother-of-pearl buttons that are my eyes and my
smile is a crescent of red thread. Five pairs of fragrant pantyhose
are bunched up for a brain (no woolgathering in this head), with
floppy forearms scissored from the heel-and-toe of socks. And at
my crotch, someone has riveted a strip of hardworking leather.

Lies only are fashioned from whole cloth. All the thinlipped
idealists and planetary diplomats could not cut and join a more
transfigured, particolored man. I should be flung forth by
rocketship to teach those misshapen strangers who patrol the
outer stars that we here on earth know how to piece together our
differences. There need be no text but textiles, the silent jigsaw
body of our beliefs. Let my mission rise above the world's
emergencies. Where I was brother to the packrat, now I shall be
kin to Christ hammered into heaven, Buddha broken on the
wheel, Mohammed strangling through the holy words on Mt.
Hira. Cargo and captain of this craft, I hurl myself inside the
mapless night, looking for a casket with a trapdoor, a cradle with
a brake.

Excursions on the Ontological Plan

Even these islands of light
Where one longs to be abandoned,
Beyond the crazed slaves and the bores
Abrading the slippage of the mind,
Darken a little at the edges—
Slub in the weedstems, gurry in the mud—
As though to remind all tourists
With a taste for cornflakes and bronze monuments
That the tea rose tilted pink against
A glaze of moonlight on palace stones
Must spread its roots deep
In dung and desire. And should one find
That each route through the hinterland
Leads to a zoo where weasels
Suck dead paint from Easter eggs,
Or to a state museum hung
With tattoos heavy in the frame, the skin
Pinpricked in savage slogans, one might well
Refuse to leave the bus, the way
Some giant fern in an arboretum
Will snub the rain, adding its slow inch
From cigar stubs and vibrations of steam.
Already the summer and the sunburnt day
Feel half rare, half done. But the shorelines
Still lap with brine as one waits

For the tide to bring back the transport
Bobbing like a bottle tossed overboard,
In which the wine dregs darken
A folded phrase of distress
Or muted alleluia, the text tainted,
Taking on the same high shade
As this navigable broth that bears up
A vexed regatta, the flags
Testing the wind or lashing out
Signals too quick to decode, as if
Plato were talking to himself again.

Acronym

I have been studying the 3000 abbreviations of sleep,
chain letters sent out from the suburbs
where children are redesigning the toothpaste tube
and lawyers stand gazing at their lawns,
afraid those strange new plumes in the high bermuda
will mean more money out the pocket, bad karma
however you look at it, and you do look
as the mailman hands you a branded envelope and steps back,
leaving you alone with those dark thoughts knocking
at the threshold of your head. Now
neither of us will understand what it means,
tired as we are from these field trips into the interior
and our late nights cataloguing
the butterflies and native labials, the broken urns
that other world was buried in; unless,
out of the acids of this life,
a dream develops like a passport photograph
that, though it in no way resembles us,
will take us pronto from this place, our footsteps
stamping down the same pavement
that welcomed us nine years before, as if time
were the solemn stiffnecked star
of the only movie that made you
drench your seat,
Revenge of the Zombies:
dead and on the move.

Deciduous Variations on Akron

Promise me something, Uncle Ray?
What?
That when I die I won't be from Ohio.
                    —Barry Hannah, *Ray*

Fall is our favorite conclusion.
We can do without
the leaves backlit from heaven,
the gold coronas, yellow of old skulls,
and reds sparking like volleys from a banjo,
in whose presence the fine-tuned hairs
of tourists vibrate and gawk.

The sky goes nowhere, a sealed confession,
the stone of Lazarus undisturbed.
We like it that way. In this tale,
the hero turns back, his horse sore-footed,
his sword heavy in his hand, never guessing
that the girl's wild cries were just
one more sad joke from the dragon.

Three wishes are never enough.
We want the axioms of autumn,
X and Y of the big trees, a natural algebra
printed on the air like
the timetable for a Chinese railway.

This is the landscape of necessity,
adventures for the ornery eye, all freaks
and flaws, aberration of atoms.

Here, the brain spins with the speed
of rearwheels in slush, snowsmoke,
the engine in a high hot whine.

And we come to the dead end
of ourselves, as if some needle pierced us
pointing out true north, the lodestar
that leads wise men to Akron—no switchbacks
or byways, no last detour
around the damage, only this white weather
where nothing changes, everything hurts.

Seasonal Adjustments

1

This winter's gone on so long
I can smell spring
even in the urinals swabbed down
with pine oil, a scent so strong
it clears a path from here
to Slidell, Louisiana
where once more I stand
moonfaced and confused
in a circle of tall trees
snarled at the top
and let the sunlight
warm me from the earth up.

2

Still north of April
and a cold rain
splinters the state, sharp
as an icepick through the heart.
I don't need this, even a blind
baffling of fog would do, something
sullen and sluggish
to hide my life in. Outside the window,

the driveway writhes with worms
and two sorry chickadees
peck at the hanging feedbox,
their wings slicked back, their skullcaps
bobbing at the seder of seeds.
What do they care
for the byzantine misery of taxes?
Their eyes don't crawl upward
when the evening news
pours its blue light on the pork chops.
They don't feel in their wet breasts
a surge, a sick fear they'll be
condemned to die in Ohio,
that last outpost of civilized asylum.
They bring back people I once knew
on the Mississippi, who loved
its loose romance, its sidle
and rich silt, its minstrel winds,
and could not spell that river's name
the same way twice.

3

I'm writing this poem
sometime before the last snowfall becomes
the first flood, each flake a wheel
spinning with my limbs
lashed to its cold spokes.
I'm writing this poem
while others defend the beachheads
of Florida, throwing their money
at the sun, bribing the sea,
living on grapefruit and degradation
I'm writing this poem
the way the ancient Persians
pursued their hard affairs,
drinking the night down
to its conclusion, then taking up
counsel again when the cups were quenched,
sober in dull daylight.
You will find this story
lodged in the nine volumes of Herodotus,
a man just Greek enough
to tell the truth
as though it were a lie
too beautiful to disbelieve.

Complaint against Complaint

All day the smallest things have turned on me—
this button swinging from my cuff
like an eyeball jarred loose; the old car confusing
second with reverse until it backs up straight ahead;
these words, tense and tired of my low-rent poems,
out scouting someplace serenely sturdy in the beams.

Now I'm looking at the way three robins
haggle over one gone worm, and the way
that spider unspools a thin shimmer in the yew,
trying to live down its bad reputation.
Now I'm letting the blood pour through the skyline
until nothing's left but the night's white knuckle.

Is it too late to call the whole show off? If he were here,
St. Francis would slide back his hood and say:
go humble through the hills and naked, where even
the bees and wolves will name you *brother*
and feed you for nothing, as if you were
too pure or stupid to forage for yourself.
But he's not here. I hoist my nuts
under the baggy bathrobe and heat the TV cuisine:
crow, with a backlash of bacon.

O when there's so much gnashing of teeth
the tongue must always be in danger. I need
some hard wine to wash this dinner down;
I need the blue haze of books and saxophones,
a muse rigged out in grit, bald,
with a bad squint; I need to know that,
whatever slurs and gripes this mouth is guilty of,
there won't be one ear listening.

THREE

If I had to live in a city I think I would prefer New Orleans to any other—both Southern and Catholic and with indications that the Devil's existence is freely recognized.

—Flannery O'Connor

Views of the Vieux Carré

We go out into
The warm unnatural morning—
Winters should be all ice
And shimmer of snow, chained wheels
Over the glassy streets—
To mail the postcards bragging
Of blue days, gumbo,
And oysters in a burlap sack,
Their slick scenes enhancing
What we saw: the white cathedral,
Arabesques of ironwork, a river
Rising out of myth and history,
Market stalls with their garlands
Of garlic and creole squash.

Friends, be grateful
For what you've got, these cards
Whose backs are too small
To hold complaint. They might be letters
Telling of homesick children
Unruly in school, motors slow
And cranky on the drive down,
An apartment of missing windowpanes
And the dead stench
Of curry dyed into the drapes.

We send you the life
It would be wrong to clarify,
A blur of bright lines, a dream
Too fluent for the facts to freeze.

Moonwalk on the Mississippi

From here the days go by like barges
That never move until I look away
And turn back to find them
Lower down the river, and wait
For the flat decks to disappear into the bend,
So distant now they must be taken on belief.

I watch them from this walkway
Reflecting the nickname of a mayor, these wooden steps
That lead me each afternoon to hear
The water wearing at the rocks, a slow return
Of stone to another state, where everything
Empties at last into the long gulf.

And I drift like those people waving
From the tourist boats, sternwheelers that browse
Through bayous under the warning eye
Of gators trolling in the standstill water, their wakes
Waning to a bank shrouded with moss.
I raise my hand to all who trespass this way.

And wherever the unspent hours wash up, in a delta
Rich with riversoil, or this crescent where spiders
Crawl from tropic cargoes on the dock, I know that
Behind me, across the statue and busy pigeons in the Square,
The cathedral clock will soon count out
The shadows striking what the sun had only touched.

—New Orleans, 1981

Hydromancy

I

I can still remember
that August when I was nine, a warm day
and mean, whitecaps building across the lake.
I had come with canepole and tackle
to the old bridge where pelicans
settled on every post to scan for mullets
catapulting near the shore. And I watched
the water turn against itself.

II

Today the surface moves like the brown sighing
of a sow's belly. I pick out a shell
from the litter on the seawall steps, a gray runt
the waves had knocked apart or the gulls broke open,
and smooth off the salt, pressing its cool shape
to my palm. There is no genius in this whorl,
these dull halfrings I rub between my fingers,
but under the winter sun something is coming true.

III

Years from now, a spring wind pants in the sail,
groaning the small boat over beer cans, gloves,
a baby in a plastic bag. Syrup of ammonia,
shawl of creosote, the lake smears beneath my face
like a window a wounded bird has thrashed against.
I don't want to raise those secrets
dragged deep in ooze, or salvage what the tides sucked out,
not while I can still remember
the end we crawled to out of mutant waters.

—Lake Pontchartrain, 1981

Fantasia on Tchoupitoulas Wharf

Some things come in their own time, as
Long before noon the stevedores, steeped
In sweat, break work for a snack
Of crackers and hogshead cheese swilled down
With cans of Dixie beer which they crush
And sail into the river, a silver tip
For the tonic of their appetites. But
Fed or fasting, they must wait for days
Before a thunderhead swells over them
Like a black toad about to croak,
The rain that comes in raw against the skin,
Steaming the gray sides of ships, and the white
Racks of lightning that force them from
Their cranes and cargo holds to the warehouse
Where money gives way to fear, where some things
Arrive before or beyond their time, and the rats
Sit out the storm while the foreman
Labors to set straight what men and weather have deranged.

Magdalena of Decatur Street

I'm no high-rise whore, I got no use
for lotions you can lick from my breasts
in six flavors like mango and crème de menthe,
no use for any Vulvamatic vibrator
with twirling attachments and touch control.

Most nights you can find me
outside the Little Dixie Bar'n'Grill,
pulling a rattail comb through my hair,
that black cloud that drizzles
an acid rain, and looking you in the eye.

All the boys know me, they call me
Queen of the Night, they buy me
those longneck beers that go down
slick as oysters off a cold shell.
But they don't know my Christian name
and I ain't telling. It's mine.

What I most like is some young one
saved up three months to meet me. And after
that first fast shot, I tease out
a second run of sperm
like rapids of wild milk, lashing and breaking.

I can bear the traffic, the catcalls,
the bulls in their seersucker suits.
It's all smoke in the bagpipes anyhow.

And at full tide I overflow
to the Greek bars, go barefoot
when the ships come in and we dance
the handkerchief dance, those small dark men
that loop and glide around me
in the midnight jukebox light, my whole body
at home, hot and fat and free, outside
the lockstep beats of the heart.

Elegy for Professor Longhair

Over the low lope of the bass, the highhat's chatter,
I'll always hear that upright
Stutter and sway—the Professor's playing
His bareknuckle rhumba boogie on Rampart Street!
Stand back now, it's the crawfish love call,
It's the wild bell ringing for resurrection,
It's the ghost of hambones in Congo Square,
Voodoo by Jesus out of Jelly Roll!

I'll take my place in the second line,
Do the zulu strut
Where the brothers sweat through the streets,
Slow drag and blues—oh the bottom
Done drop out the big drum and the horn's
All empty, but the tourists still
Step off the train, some hi-fi squalling
Get yo' ticket in yo' hand, you wanna go to New Orleans!

I've come back and you've gone.
No gospel or gris-gris
Could keep you here, however much
You loved the jukejoints pouring out
Bourbon and a smoky beat, the palm trees
Lashing their green rhythm down Elysian Fields.
These words are for the wide river
That spreads forever south, and that black box

You rode like a raft into heaven.

Plantation

Now, at dusk, beyond the river's slow strokes
and the migraine of mosquitoes, I almost see
her white gown glide across the columns, a silk bell
that echoes down the long alley of pine and oak
where on her bridal day she walked beneath
a gold and silver tangle in the branches, a dust
the field slaves spread through the canopy of webs
hung by spiders her father shipped from Africa.

Now, under the snags of moss, a small wind
rises from that hollow of brick and cypress beams,
too weak to blow the ghosts away, though it carries
a bobwhite's call from the canebrake, the dry stalks
that rattle like chains, and from the worn earth it brings
a lolling odor of jasmine and black sweat.

What life do I betray, standing here
on the false side of history, facing two pasts
beyond approach: these ruins the moon will overflow
and, far behind, those sour cabins gone back to darkness
under the wild grass, the spearhead blades of palmetto?
Now, at the edge of judgment, I lean against
a rough pine stuck with locust pods split down the back,
and enter this long moment haunting the bottomland, a bitter
beauty that seven generations could not raze forever or restore.

Mosquito Hawks

You call them dragonflies
But you come from another country
Of snow and unions, without a summer
Worth the name. I passed my childhood
Picking them off the wire fence
That kept my father's junkyard
From my mother's house, and bringing them
Back to the concrete slab—both morgue
And front porch—where my brother
Waited to probe them with a pin,
Their fierce heads turning like ball-turrets
To attack the thin pain suddenly inside them.
It was soon done, the jaws snapped open
Forever and the wings swept down
A final time. The matchbox burials
Bored us before long—science
Never weeps over those martyrs whose reward
Is the walking lame, the robot heart,
The comatose who go on living.

Your young days were different—
You would lie down for hours in August
Behind the family's weekend home
(Three bathrooms, a deck foursquare to the sun),

Watching them patrol the dusk
For insects, the sheer panels of their wings
Holding the light's last color, a fire so distant
It burns only in fables now.

Darling, whatever name they died under,
It was an old story we repeated
Years ago, your privilege always to witness
Those brave banners that take the field
And never to hear
The rebel yells surpassing sure defeat.

Cajun Graveyard

You must go beyond
those old square slat-sided homes
where dead leaves stumble down the street

and blue runners bend across the sugardirt
like the tires of bicycles
torn in two,

and find yourself
halfway to nowhere,
the ground sucking underfoot

as if to pull you in,
a siege of water
that slows down the land.

If you were seeking
enigmas in the stone,
the graveyard stone of northern colonies,

there are none here, no lives
that might be rubbed away
and framed against a parlor wall—

only stoneflies that spin a lazy loop
around the sun and bristle
through the toadflax and Spanish dagger.

Each plot ends
in a slant moss-branded cross,
silvered by the wind and rain,

propped up with
boxes of the dead,
those pine contraptions

where, under lids of glass,
someone has wired in backwood designs
of brooding beads, jewelled insects,

and unnatural eyes
that stare so deep and cold
you turn your head away.

The stories here are carried
in the heart, not blazoned out
for passing strangers: that heavy man

standing by the white chaplets
of bridal wreath can tell you
how in this bog was buried

his *grandpère*'s neighbor
lost to the *loup-garou;*
and over there a gambler burns

who took with him to the grave
his charm for bottom cards,
the ninth bone of a black cat's tail;

and back to where the high grass
blows all day without a breeze,
he points out his wife still withers

like the fish bouquet she lies beneath,
mean as catfish, a sweetmeat snack
for beetles and the muddy slugs.

From far off as
False River and St. Francisville,
they all come back to

the parish they had cradled in
and could not finally leave.
Under your eggshell tread,

these souls, these dreams
in remission
before the cure that kills,

wash inside the soil, not like
the ghostly air of swampgas, that fraud
fading on the green dawn, but like

the wild stirrings
from grass-spike to weed-stalk
that send you trembling into your own new skin.

High Ground in Louisiana

Women are walking on the levee, up where
The winds brush cool against them

Even in August, clinging their dresses tightly
Around thighs, bare feet freshened in the grass.

They feel the river push beneath them,
Muscle of water that lifts the great freighters

Towards Africa or the crooked streets of Europe,
Worlds away from the brown bayous sleeping

Under their fathers' boats, so still
They could hear the catfish snore. At the green hour,

Young women simmer in the breeze and sweep
Their long hair back with ribbons, loving

The slow bulge of ships that leave them
Shaken like the heat, the waves of day dissolving.

Chicken on Sunday

Sometimes, thinking about women,
I call back those Sundays
When the black man my father paid
Would hold a red hen's head
Across the block and with an axe
Hack it clean through, the carcass
Scrabbling in the gravel, its soul
A wild spray in the face. And
Wiping my eyes free, I'd watch him
Scald the body deep
Inside a pail, his big hands
Stripping the craw down to skin,
The blue slops and grit gouged out.
It was the edge of revelation, like Swift
Sick that the great globes
Of Celia's ass could shit. And we'd eat
The flesh my mother set before us,
White meat and dark, my mouth
Pulling at the bird, its thin wings
And wishbone bent back, its small heart
Still steaming on the platter, a scrap
My tongue could never take to, dry
Hole of darkness, gristle at the lips.

Cottonmouth

On the mud shore at Mandeville,
Summer swarming around me, I stepped
Halfway up a cypress knee to watch

The stale waves collapsing on the lake,
And then put both feet firmly down
To straddle the crooked root. Nearby,

The driftwood slid in a slow turn;
One black branch untangled itself
And twisted free. Long and round

As a dwarf's leg, the blunt body
Spilled forward in my direction, stopping
Where my left shoe scuffed the mud.

I could not shift or scream, afraid
The squat loops would straighten out
And slip again into power glide.

When the hinges of the jaw dropped open,
I looked into a bomber's moon, two teeth
Filling their tunnels with bad milk.

And I saw myself stretched out stiff
In that casket of odd cotton, held in
By the twin hooks of pain and repose.

The slant eyes locked on mine, cold
As the gunmetal scales overcast along
The stubborn stump that bent against my life.

I did not blink, though sweat streamed
In currents from my forehead, both of us stinking
With the hot musk of the swampland,

Both bewildered, too brooding to risk
Another inch forward or away. If my lips
Had not fused shut with fear,

I could have called for a club
To crush that catastrophic head,
And let the venom drizzle in the mud.

He would not strike; I could not stir—
Until, like a comic scene relieving
The heartstop of tragedy, a vagrant turtle

Picked its slow way out of the marsh
To gawk at the standoff, its oldman's neck
Telescoping from the shell for a better look.

And in that stretched second
Of the snake's distraction,
I pulled free from the treeroot,

Leaving one life behind me
On the beach, and another
Walking backward into the future.

At Bay St. Louis

No wind, even the sun in irons,
And the telltales lagging down the stays—
The whole heavy afternoon stalls to a trance.

I keep a tired course across the bay, one leg
Looped over the hiking stick, one hand
Tracing the saltscrawls of water below the boat.

Voyageur, voyeur: I watch as you disband
The halter and press into the deck, your breasts
Spread warm beneath you in a slow blur.

Summer and sleep. Nostalgias of the flesh.
Will this day never waken or breathe again,
Or the sky break through its deep coma of clouds?

I drift back to that night of port and panatelas,
A candle tapping its flame against the dark
And in your room the whispers fading.

By starlight and shadow, we knew the world was bent
On its own way, its good turns pulling us down
Until your name was fire in my mouth.

Now all those years have come to water,
The stubborn water that stays us, two salt hearts at Bay
St. Louis where the horizon draws a line

Over the harbor, the slip we sailed from
Before the day was wasted in dead weather.
That is another shore we'll never reach.

Wading the Gulf

I still see you spilled out
in the low waters off Biloxi, the gulf stream
warming itself on your thighs.

That night was a steeple of stars
and the poisoned bells
of jellyfish floating down the dark.

What were you thinking then,
a half mile out from shore
where the water's soiled silk

still only tugged between our legs,
your breasts set free
in a blue permission of the moon?

Did you want those salt shallows
to plummet sudden, deep, and cold,
your face dissolving in the brine?

That night for the first time
I felt my birth
wash round me again, and looked out

over the stalled sea,
that foolish soup I stewed in
before some fish

stood on its hind fins and suckcd
a new self from the air.
Far behind us, bonfires

leaped on the beach
like signal flares to call us back,
as if we were the ones lost.

Possum County Breakdown

Driving through even the most coonbent, stumpwater
outlands of the South, you can see
these hovels crazy with azaleas,
accelerating into beauty. In the front yard,
three children squat in a ring, barefoot
and strangling the cat whose past catastrophes
have already emptied his mean brain
and earned him the name he never answered to:
Mulehead. No one minds if you sit there
drinking drugstore bourbon behind the wheel,
letting each hard pull improve the drama.
Then it's twilight on the back roads, slow seep of moon
and all the hormones hopping like frogs
in a spring ditch, big-eyed and amok.
Pa swings home from his daywork,
the dragtail dog at his heels; he's humming
a little gospel tune he can't recall the words to,
though they must be true and everlasting
like the woman who waits for him upside
the doorpost, brushing down from her wobbly hair
a black natter of gnats. Well, that looks good.
And in the flare from a hurricane lamp
you can just make out their moist daughter
pressing her thin dress to the windowpane—
and she's the darling of your dreams!

Half-stoned and moaning, your heart
rattling like a woodpecker's honeymoon,
you take her where the neon rubs against the night
from motels blinking out their prices, and she says
yes yes and all you want, as if this were really happening
and you could hold her helpless in your arms,
hot crust of her nipples upswept as she
brands your unclaimed hide. . . .
And you wake to those wild kids
whanging on your fenders, those red-dirt dwarfs
an eyelash away from idiots, and know
that feeling, the sweat sick on your forehead,
as if you had just stepped out of a film's false darkness
into the disappointing light of day.

Red Beans & Rice

This town is full of Tabasco
and clarinet players named Sidney,
grasshopper ethics with a catfish smile.
We are always kind to strangers, because
that's where the money comes from—greenbacks
gushing out of Dallas, a trickle of small change
from Toledo. Even the clouds cooperate,
backing up when the sun wants an easement
or rushing rain down to keep the oysters happy.
We measure love on a sliding scale, not like
those hardshell women and peckerwoods upstate
where nobody sucks on grain liquor and bangs
the bottom of a lard can while the radio
cracks out another sloppy chorus of Frogman Henry
crooning "Is You Is Or Is You Ain't My Baby?"
But come Sunday, we balance on our knees,
strippers and street cleaners in the same pew, listening
with our heads shut tight so the sermon
won't use up the rest of the week. The other days, too,
have their mottoes and regalia: Mondays are made
for sidemeat steaming on a mound of rice
and red beans, the ugly child that only his mother loves;
Tuesday breaks once a year, a fat riot, a freaks' parade
before forty slow days of denial; Wednesday stays home,

a bubble of nothing dead center
in the spirit level; Thursdays blunder around
like a blind paraplegic on a whoopee crutch,
no cure except suicide or Friday, when seafood
heals whatever hurts us: okra gumbo for the dispossessed,
blue crabs and crawfish for the idiots, fantail shrimp
spread out to ease the insulted and the injured.
And Saturday nights, thank God, we all get sick again.
If summer's hot scenes make us too lazy
to live, we don't mind, the funerals here
are worth dying for—a ruckus of bells and old priests
praying for cool weather in the afterlife, and sometimes
the wild umbrellas, drumgrunts and trumpets
of a streetband raising the dust, the whole spook show
swinging through laments as a limousine
drives off to deposit you in a vault guarded by
a stone angel standing on the roof, his heavy wings
closed behind him like the last exit out of paradise.

—New Orleans, 1981

The Iowa Poetry Prize Winners

1988
Elton Glaser, *Tropical Depressions*
Michael Pettit, *Cardinal Points*

Elton Glaser teaches at the University of Akron. His first book, *Relics,* was published by Wesleyan University Press in 1984.